Introduction to Vibe Coding

Ditch the Boilerplate, Embrace the Flow

Author: Thomas DeGan

◼ Introduction to *Vibe Coding: Ditch the Boilerplate, Embrace the Flow*

How to Build Software with AI Code Generators — No Matter Your Experience Level

💬 PART I: VIBING WITH CODE — A WHOLE NEW WAVE

Chapter 1: Welcome to the Vibe

- The rise of AI-assisted coding
- What "vibe coding" really means
- How this changes the way we build software
- Why anyone — coder or not — can get started today

Chapter 2: From Code Monkeys to Code DJs

- A short history of how we got here
- Traditional coding vs. vibe coding
- Programming as orchestration, not construction
- Why "flow" matters more than syntax

Chapter 3: Meet the Machines — AI Code Tools That Vibe With You

- Overview of top AI code tools:

  - **GitHub Copilot**
  - **ChatGPT (OpenAI)**
  - **Cursor**
  - **Replit Ghostwriter**
  - **Cody (Sourcegraph)**
  - **Claude (Anthropic)**
  - **bolt.new**

- VS Code, Cursor, browser-based setups, and CLIs
- Using multiple LLMs for better output
- Plugins, extensions, and automations

Chapter 8: Code by Conversation — Use Cases in Action

- CRUD apps and REST APIs
- Front-end magic: React, Vue, Svelte
- Mobile apps (React Native, Flutter)
- Full-stack builds with bolt.new or lovable.dev
- Using AI to generate docs, tests, and data mocks

Chapter 9: Debugging with a Digital Sidekick

- Using AI to find and explain bugs
- Teaching the AI your code context
- Code smells, refactors, and performance tuning
- Staying in control — when AI goes rogue

🚀 PART IV: BUILDING AND SHIPPING IN THE AI ERA

Chapter 10: Start with Just an Idea

- Building apps from pure language
- From whiteboard to working prototype
- Project walkthrough: a to-do app with a twist
- Teaching non-devs to launch with AI

Chapter 11: Scaling the Vibe — Big Projects, Small Teams

- AI as a junior dev, mentor, and PM
- Managing scope and versioning with AI
- Scaffolding, component generation, and modular design
- Team workflows when everyone's vibing

Chapter 12: Deploy, Launch, Repeat

- AI-assisted deployment and CI/CD
- Packaging, shipping, and marketing with AI
- Maintaining and evolving your product
- Building in public — with your AI copilot

🌐 PART V: WHERE WE'RE HEADED

Chapter 13: Will Everyone Be a Developer?

- Democratization of coding
- Devs as product designers, strategists, and artists
- What happens when the line between code and idea disappears?

Chapter 14: Staying Human in an AI World

- Guardrails, ethics, and hallucinations
- Open source, IP concerns, and trust
- Why your taste, intuition, and imagination still matter

Chapter 15: Your Vibe Coding Journey

- How to stay sharp, inspired, and evolving
- Communities, forums, and resources
- Building your own workflows, toolchains, and habits
- Keep vibing — and help others start, too

🔗 Appendices

- **A. Prompt Templates** — Ready-to-use structures for common dev tasks

- **B. Glossary of Terms** — LLM, prompt chaining, hallucination, etc.
- **C. 10 Projects to Try Right Now** — Buildable in a weekend with AI tools
- **D. Resources & Communities** — Where to keep learning and connecting

PART I: VIBING WITH CODE — A WHOLE NEW WAVE

Chapter 1: Welcome to the Vibe

"Don't write code. Describe the vibe."
— Andrej Karpathy

🧠 The Rise of AI-Assisted Coding

There's a quiet revolution happening in software development — and chances are, you're already seeing it.

The command line is no longer the only gateway to building apps. Today, developers are handing over the grunt work — the boilerplate, the config files, the repetitive functions — to **AI code generators**. And it's not just devs. **Anyone** with a clear idea and a bit of curiosity can start building.

At the heart of this shift is the idea of **collaborative creation**. You're no longer the machine's operator — you're its **creative partner**. You tell it what you want to build, it drafts something, and you shape it into reality. That's the vibe.

🎧 What "Vibe Coding" Really Means

When AI researcher **Andrej Karpathy** dropped the term "vibe coding," it immediately clicked for thousands of developers.

Here's the idea:

- You don't need to write every line of code.

- You describe what you want — in **natural language**.
- The AI generates code for you — fast.
- Your job is to **guide, test, tweak**, and keep the vision on track.

It's not "no-code" — it's **high-level code direction**.
It's not lazy — it's **efficient creativity**.
It's not magic — but it sure feels close.

🖊 Prompt Walkthrough: "Give Me a Rocket Button"

Prompt (in plain English):

```
Create an HTML + JavaScript snippet with a button
labeled 'Launch Rockets'. When clicked, it should
trigger a rocket launch animation using CSS.
```

What the AI gives back:

```html
<!DOCTYPE html>
<html>
<head>
  <style>
    .rocket {
      position: relative;
      top: 100px;
      transition: top 1s ease-out;
    }
    .rocket.launch {
      top: -200px;
    }
  </style>
```

```
</head>
<body>
  <button onclick="launchRocket()">Launch
Rockets</button>
  <img src="rocket.png" class="rocket" id="rocket"
width="100" />

  <script>
    function launchRocket() {

document.getElementById('rocket').classList.add('launch
');
    }
  </script>
</body>
</html>
```

💥 That's the vibe — a full working prototype from a sentence. No Googling. No Stack Overflow. Just your idea → app.

◼ How This Changes the Way We Build Software

Traditional coding used to be about:

- Remembering syntax
- Choosing frameworks
- Managing files and folders
- Writing every function by hand

Now? It's about:

- Communicating clearly

- Thinking in **systems**, not just code
- Prompting, testing, and refining
- Using your brain for vision, not repetition

Vibe coding flips the script:

- You're the **director**, not the grip.
- You build faster, learn faster, and stay in flow.
- You let the AI handle the grunt work while you **steer the ship**.

● Why Anyone — Coder or Not — Can Start Today

Here's the thing most people don't realize:
You don't need to be a professional dev to start building real, working software anymore.

Who can use vibe coding?

- **Startup founders**: Ship your MVP without waiting for a CTO.
- **Designers**: Turn UI ideas into working frontends.
- **Freelancers**: Move faster, deliver more.
- **Beginners**: Learn by *building* instead of memorizing.
- **Non-coders**: Generate backend logic, deploy apps, and learn on the fly.

If you can think clearly and express what you want, **you can build with AI**.

✏ Prompt Walkthrough: Create a To-Do API

Prompt:

```
Create an Express.js REST API for managing to-do items.
```

Include GET, POST, PUT, and DELETE endpoints. Store the items in memory.

AI Response:

```javascript
const express = require('express');
const app = express();
app.use(express.json());

let todos = [];
let id = 1;

app.get('/todos', (req, res) => res.json(todos));

app.post('/todos', (req, res) => {
  const todo = { id: id++, text: req.body.text };
  todos.push(todo);
  res.status(201).json(todo);
});

app.put('/todos/:id', (req, res) => {
  const todo = todos.find(t => t.id == req.params.id);
  if (todo) {
    todo.text = req.body.text;
    res.json(todo);
  } else {
    res.status(404).send('Not found');
  }
});

app.delete('/todos/:id', (req, res) => {
  todos = todos.filter(t => t.id != req.params.id);
  res.status(204).send();
```

```
});

app.listen(3000, () => console.log('API running on port
3000'));
```

In under 30 seconds, you've got a backend for a full-stack app — even
if you've never built one before.

■ The Big Takeaways

- Vibe coding is here — and it's changing how we create
  software.
- AI code tools let you build fast, using **natural language and
  intention**.
- You don't need years of experience — just a vision and a
  prompt.
- You're still in control. The AI writes code, **you steer the vibe**.

✗ Coming Up Next

In **Chapter 2: From Code Monkeys to Code DJs**, we'll dig into how
we got here — from manual coding to frameworks to full-on AI
collaboration — and why this moment is a turning point in tech history.

Chapter 2: From Code Monkeys to Code DJs

🎋 A Short History of How We Got Here

To understand **vibe coding**, it helps to know what came before. Programming has always been about getting a machine to do what you want — but the way we *talk* to machines has changed a lot.

◼ The Manual Era

- Think punch cards, assembly language, and pure C.
- Developers had to control *everything* — memory, CPU, timing.
- Creativity was there, but it was buried under layers of technical friction.

◼ The Framework Era

- Languages like Python, JavaScript, and Ruby made things friendlier.
- Frameworks like React, Django, and Rails gave us scaffolding.
- But it was still *code-first*: you had to learn the rules to play the game.

🤖 The AI Era (Where We Are Now)

- Natural language is the new API.
- Tools like **ChatGPT**, **GitHub Copilot**, **Cursor**, and **bolt.new** let you build with your words.
- The shift? From construction to **orchestration**.

🏛 Traditional Coding vs. Vibe Coding

Let's break this down:

Traditional Coding	Vibe Coding
Write every line manually	Describe what you want in plain English
Learn syntax + framework rules	Focus on outcomes and intent
Lots of boilerplate + setup	AI handles the setup + scaffolding
You vs. the docs	You + AI working together
Tedious debugging	Conversational debugging with AI
Time-intensive iterations	Fast prototyping and feedback loops

🎼 Programming as Orchestration, Not Construction

Vibe coding isn't about writing *less* code — it's about writing **higher-level code**.

You're still building systems. You still need logic, structure, and clarity. But you're doing it by *conducting* the code, not hammering it out line by line.

- You describe a REST API → AI writes the endpoints.
- You sketch a UI in text → AI builds the layout.
- You test a bug fix → AI suggests the patch.

It's a **collaborative composition**. Think:

- You = the **conductor**
- The AI = your **orchestra**
- The code = your **music**

The more clearly you direct, the better the performance.

⚡ Why "Flow" Matters More Than Syntax

There's this magical state all creatives know: **flow**.

It's when:

- You lose track of time.
- Ideas come naturally.
- You're building, iterating, moving — without friction.

Traditional coding interrupts flow constantly:

- "Why is this import not working?"
- "What's the right syntax for this array method?"
- "Where's that piece of documentation again?"

Vibe coding removes those roadblocks. It keeps you **in the zone**:

- Less Googling.
- Fewer distractions.
- More *doing*.

When you can think in outcomes — and the AI translates that into functioning software — you stay locked in the creative cycle longer.

And that's where the best work happens.

🗨 Code Example: Flowing into a Signup Page

Let's say you're building a signup page. In traditional coding, you might Google the form markup, validation logic, and figure out how to wire it into your backend.

With vibe coding:

Prompt:

```
Create a signup form in HTML and JavaScript with fields
for name, email, and password. Include basic validation
and show an alert on successful submission.
```

AI Response:

```html
<form id="signupForm">
  <input type="text" id="name" placeholder="Name"
required /><br />
  <input type="email" id="email" placeholder="Email"
required /><br />
  <input type="password" id="password"
placeholder="Password" required /><br />
  <button type="submit">Sign Up</button>
</form>

<script>

document.getElementById("signupForm").addEventListener(
```

```
"submit", function(e) {
    e.preventDefault();
    const name = document.getElementById("name").value;
    const email =
document.getElementById("email").value;
    const password =
document.getElementById("password").value;

    if (!name || !email || !password) {
      alert("Please fill in all fields.");
    } else {
      alert(`Welcome, ${name}!`);
    }
  });
</script>
```

Instant form. No documentation rabbit hole. No Stack Overflow loop. Just **flow**.

■ Recap: From Monkeys to DJs

- Coding used to be about constructing every piece manually.
- Now it's about **directing**, prompting, and remixing — like a DJ with beats.
- The AI doesn't replace your brain — it frees it up.
- Focus on flow, not friction.
- Think in systems, not syntax.

You're not just writing code anymore. You're conducting it.

🎧 Up Next: Chapter 3 — *Meet the Machines: AI Code Tools That Vibe With You*

In the next chapter, we'll meet the tools behind this movement — from Copilot to Cursor to bolt.new and beyond. You'll learn what they're best at, how they differ, and how to mix them for your own workflow.

Chapter 3: Meet the Machines — AI Code Tools That Vibe With You

---

You're not coding alone anymore — you've got a squad of digital collaborators.

🤖 The AI Renaissance in Development Tools

We're living in an *AI tool boom*. New platforms are dropping every week, all aimed at one thing: **making it easier, faster, and more fun to build software**.

These tools aren't just productivity boosters — they're **co-creators**, helping you write code, debug it, refactor it, test it, and sometimes even deploy it. But not all tools do the same thing. Each has its vibe.

So let's meet the lineup.

⚙️ The Core Vibe Coders

1. GitHub Copilot

- **Type**: Inline code generator

- **Vibe**: Quiet genius whispering code as you type
- **Best for**: Autocomplete inside VS Code or JetBrains; great at repetitive logic, boilerplate, and known patterns

Strengths:

- Context-aware suggestions
- Supports multiple languages
- Feels invisible (in a good way)

Use when: You're coding inside a project and want to speed up flow without changing tools.

2. ChatGPT (OpenAI)

- **Type**: Conversational assistant + code generator
- **Vibe**: Your nerdy best friend who never sleeps
- **Best for**: Asking "how do I...?" questions, writing whole chunks of code, debugging, code reviews, and learning

Strengths:

- Excellent for explanations and iterative prompts
- Can maintain state within a conversation
- Works well for learning and experimentation

Use when: You're exploring a new idea, stuck on a concept, or need detailed guidance.

3. Cursor

- **Type**: AI-native code editor
- **Vibe**: Coding in the future, today

- **Best for**: Editing entire projects with context-aware AI; refactoring, debugging, and deep code reasoning

Strengths:

- Integrates ChatGPT directly into your codebase
- Understands file context and dependencies
- Ideal for real projects, not just code snippets

Use when: You want a VS Code-style IDE powered by AI that "gets" your project structure.

4. Replit Ghostwriter

- **Type**: Browser-based AI IDE
- **Vibe**: Fast, accessible, and instant feedback
- **Best for**: Building quick prototypes, solo hacker projects, beginners learning to code

Strengths:

- Real-time collaboration
- Browser-based — no setup
- Great for education and live coding

Use when: You want to move fast, code in the cloud, or experiment in a low-friction space.

5. Cody (by Sourcegraph)

- **Type**: AI for large codebases
- **Vibe**: The archivist who remembers everything

- **Best for**: Understanding legacy code, navigating huge projects, generating smart diffs and summaries

Strengths:

- Built to scale with big teams
- Deep code analysis and memory
- Works with self-hosted environments

Use when: You're working in a team or on a massive repo and need AI to help you think big.

6. Claude (Anthropic)

- **Type**: Conversational assistant
- **Vibe**: The calm philosopher with a massive memory
- **Best for**: Writing and reasoning over large blocks of code or text

Strengths:

- 100K+ token context window
- Good at summarizing or refactoring large files
- Polished and safe output

Use when: You need long-form reasoning, big-code summarization, or gentle code reviews.

7. bolt.new

- **Type**: Idea-to-product builder
- **Vibe**: One prompt and done

- **Best for**: Turning product ideas into working full-stack prototypes — fast

Strengths:

- Full-stack app generation
- Beautiful UX
- Especially useful for solo devs, founders, and makers

Use when: You want to turn an idea into a working MVP in a weekend.

8. lovable.dev

- **Type**: UI-first app builder
- **Vibe**: The no-code builder with AI power under the hood
- **Best for**: Designers and non-coders building real apps visually with AI guidance

Strengths:

- UI-focused
- AI suggests backends, logic, and flows
- Great for people who think in visuals

Use when: You want to build without touching code — or mix visual and AI-driven workflows.

🏆 Honorable Mentions

Tool	What it does well

Codeium	Fast autocomplete, lightweight setup
Tabnine	ML-based code suggestions, privacy-first
AskCodi	Prompt-based coding + documentation generation
Continue	Local AI models + open-source IDE extensions
Phind	AI-enhanced search and code snippets

🔴 When to Use What — Strengths & Sweet Spots

Goal	Best Tool(s)
Writing boilerplate code fast	GitHub Copilot, Cursor
Building full apps from ideas	bolt.new, ChatGPT, lovable.dev

Debugging or fixing bugs	Cursor, Claude, ChatGPT
Refactoring or summarizing code	Claude, Cody
Working on a massive project	Cody, Cursor
Prototyping in the browser	Replit Ghostwriter
Visual design to app	lovable.dev

Why Pairing Tools Is a Superpower

Real talk: **you don't need to choose one**.

Some of the best workflows involve **mixing tools**:

- Use **ChatGPT** to plan your app → Use **Copilot** to implement it.
- Use **Claude** to refactor messy code → Use **Cursor** to test changes.
- Design in **lovable.dev** → Extend backend logic with **bolt.new**.
- Use **Cody** to understand a legacy codebase → Use **ChatGPT** to rewrite pieces.

You're not locked into one assistant. You're building a **dream team**.

And as new tools emerge, your AI toolbox only gets stronger.

■ Chapter Recap

- There's a tool for every coding vibe.
- Some are great for UI, some for APIs, some for massive codebases.
- Don't marry one — **mix, match, and flow**.
- The best devs aren't just good coders — they're good *conductors* of the tools around them.

🚀 Up Next: Chapter 4 — *You're Not Coding, You're Conducting*

Next chapter, we'll dig deeper into the shift from "coder" to "conductor." We'll explore how your role evolves when AI handles the syntax, and what new skills matter in this new era of building.

PART II: MASTERING THE VIBE CODING MINDSET

Chapter 4: You're Not Coding, You're Conducting

"The future developer isn't the one who types faster — it's the one who thinks clearer."

The New Role of the Developer

The vibe coder isn't just someone who "codes with AI."
They're someone who **thinks like a conductor**.

- They don't write every note — they guide the orchestra.
- They don't obsess over every symbol — they focus on harmony.
- They stay in the flow, making creative choices, not mechanical ones.

In the past, being a "good developer" often meant:

- Memorizing syntax
- Learning frameworks inside-out
- Writing clean, efficient code by hand

But vibe coding changes the game:

- It's not about how much code you write — it's how well you **frame your ideas**
- It's not about knowing every detail — it's about knowing what matters

- It's less about being a technician, more about being a **creative systems thinker**

🧠 Framing Your Intent for the Machine

In vibe coding, the most important skill isn't technical — it's **communicative clarity**.

When you work with an AI like ChatGPT, Claude, or Copilot, you're doing something powerful:
You're translating **human intent** into something a machine can act on.

That means your job shifts from writing this:

```
function add(a, b) {
   return a + b;
}
```

To saying this:

```
Create a function that takes two numbers and returns
their sum.
```

But it goes deeper. Here's a scale of intent clarity:

🧠 Level	Example Prompt

🔺 Vague	"Make a cool app."
🔍 Focused	"Build a React app that displays weather data using the OpenWeather API."
⚫ Crystal Clear	"Create a responsive React app with a search input that fetches and displays weather info for a given city using the OpenWeather API. Show temperature, humidity, and an icon for the weather condition. Use TailwindCSS for styling."

The more clearly you express your **vision**, the better the AI performs.

⚫ Tip Box: How to Think Like a Vibe Coder

- **✳️ Break big ideas into parts**
  → APIs, UI, state logic, and testing
- **🔨 Describe the outcome you want**
  → Not how to code it, but what it should do
- **⬛ Iterate and refine**
  → The first result is the start, not the finish
- **✏️ Talk to the AI like a teammate**
  → "Can you improve this?" is totally valid
- **🧘 Let go of control (sometimes)**
  → Great things happen when you trust the flow

🔭 Zooming Out: Thinking in Systems, Not Just Lines

One of the most powerful mindset shifts in vibe coding is learning to **zoom out**.

Traditional coding often pulls you into details:

- "Is this the right syntax?"
- "Where should I put this component?"
- "What's the error in this function?"

Vibe coding invites you to zoom out and ask:

- "What is this feature trying to do?"
- "How do the parts of this app connect?"
- "How can I explain this to an AI clearly?"

Instead of obsessing over implementation, you start architecting the **whole experience**.

> 🧩 You move from "What should this function return?"
> ⬛ To "How does this feature serve the user?"

That's a massive upgrade. That's where flow lives.

✏️ Real Example: Planning a Note-Taking App

Instead of diving into code, you start like this:

Prompt:

Help me plan a simple web-based note-taking app.

I want to:

- Allow users to create, edit, and delete notes

- Store notes in the browser with localStorage

- Use vanilla JavaScript and minimal CSS

- Keep the UI clean and mobile-friendly

The AI gives back:

- Suggested file structure
- A list of features
- A working code scaffold

From there, you iterate:

- "Add a search bar to filter notes by keyword."
- "Add timestamps to each note."
- "Style it with a minimalist theme."

You're not trapped in the code anymore — **you're building the system**.

◼ Chapter Recap

- Vibe coders are **conductors**, not typists
- Your role is to **communicate clearly and think big**
- Clarity of intent beats syntax perfection
- Zoom out, think in **systems**, and stay in the flow

- AI isn't a crutch — it's a **creative amplifier**

🚀 Up Next: Chapter 5 — *The Art of Prompting*

We're about to get practical. In the next chapter, you'll learn the actual craft of writing great prompts — how to speak to AI in a way that gets you what you want, faster and better.

Chapter 5: The Art of Prompting

"Prompting is programming in vibe coding — but instead of syntax, you're writing intent."

🔥 Crafting Clear, Powerful Prompts

In vibe coding, **prompting is the main skill**. It's how you communicate your vision to an AI — the clearer your prompt, the better the output.

Think of a prompt like a conversation starter:

- Too vague? You'll get a vague answer.
- Too specific? You might over-constrain it.
- Just right? The AI flows with you.

🔑 The Prompting Sweet Spot:

1. **State the goal**
2. **Define the context**
3. **Describe the desired output**
4. **(Optional) Add constraints or preferences**

💡 Prompt Makeover Example:

❌ Weak Prompt:

```
Make a login system.
```

Strong Prompt:

```
Create a secure login form in HTML and JavaScript with
fields for email and password. Add basic client-side
validation and show an alert on successful login. No
backend -- just front-end logic.
```

Notice how the second one is:

- Specific
- Scoped
- Outcome-driven

🧩 Prompt Structures for Different Dev Tasks

Let's break down how to prompt for **specific purposes**.

🧱 1. Writing Code

Structure:

```
Write [functionality] using [language/framework].
Include [features or constraints].
```

Example:

```
Write a Node.js function that sends a POST request to a
webhook URL with JSON data containing a username and
timestamp.
```

🖊 2. Debugging Code

Structure:

```
I'm getting [error] in this code.
Explain what's going wrong and how to fix it.
[Paste code]
```

Example:

```
I'm getting "undefined is not a function" when calling
map().
Can you explain why?
[Paste array code]
```

🖊 3. Writing Tests

Structure:

```
Generate unit tests for the following function using
[testing library].
[Paste function]
```

Example:

```
Write Jest tests for this function that checks if a
string is a palindrome.
```

✓ 4. Refactoring

Structure:

```
Refactor this code to make it more
[readable/performant/DRY].
[Paste code]
```

Example:

```
Refactor this React component to reduce repetition and
improve readability.
```

5. Generating Docs

Structure:

```
Generate a README for this project based on the
following code and its features.
[Paste code or describe features]
```

6. Code Reviews

Structure:

```
Act as a code reviewer.
Analyze this function for readability, security, and
performance.
[Paste code]
```

Iterative Prompting, Chaining, and Creative Remixing

Prompting is a *process*, not a one-shot trick. Great vibe coders:

- Ask → Read → Refine → Re-ask → Remix

Example: Iterative Workflow

Step 1 — Starter Prompt:

```
Create a REST API for managing tasks in Express.
```

Step 2 — After seeing the code:

```
Nice. Now add in-memory storage with IDs for each task.
```

Step 3 — Next refinement:

```
Add input validation to make sure each task has a name
and description.
```

Step 4 — Final touch:

```
Add error handling with proper status codes and
messages.
```

This is **prompt chaining** — breaking up the request into layers and building complexity step by step. It's how you stay in flow and in control.

🦅 Prompt Remixing: Turn One Idea Into Many

You can reuse and remix prompts to go further:

- Turn a code snippet into tests
- Turn a test into documentation
- Turn a function into a UI component

Example:

```
Take this Express route and generate a matching
frontend form using React.
```

Or:

```
Now generate unit tests for this form's validation
logic.
```

You're not just asking for code — you're **building a system, piece by piece**, across layers.

🍃 Prompt Templates for Real-World Use Cases

Use Case	Prompt Template
Build a Feature	"Build a [feature] using [tech]. Include [requirements]."
Fix a Bug	"This code throws an error: [error]. Fix and explain it."

Explain Something	"Explain how [tech/concept] works using simple language and examples."
Write Tests	"Write [test type] for this code using [framework]."
Refactor Code	"Refactor this to be cleaner/more performant/more secure."
Plan a Project	"Help me plan a [project type] with [tools]. Give me a basic file structure, features, and setup steps."

■ Chapter Recap

- Great prompting = great output
- Be clear, be specific, and guide the AI like a creative partner
- Use templates to speed up your work
- Don't expect magic on the first try — prompt iteratively
- Prompting is a skill — and it's the most valuable one in the AI dev toolkit

🚀 Up Next: Chapter 6 — *Flow State Coding*

Now that you've got the tools and the language, we're going to explore what it *feels* like to code in flow — with real examples, mini builds, and strategies for staying in the creative zone with your AI copilot.

Chapter 6: Flow State Coding

"Flow is when time disappears, the cursor moves like magic, and your idea becomes a living, breathing app."

🎵 Recognizing and Harnessing "The Vibe"

If you've ever hit that moment where everything just clicks — where the ideas flow, the code works, and you lose track of time — **you've felt the flow state**.

In traditional coding, hitting that state often takes hours of setup, refactoring, and mental warm-up. In **vibe coding**, you can enter it almost instantly.

That's the magic of it:

- No boilerplate.
- No config spirals.
- No documentation black holes.
- Just: *Describe → Generate → Build → Repeat.*

Flow State in Vibe Coding looks like:

- Chatting with AI like it's your teammate
- Rapidly going from idea to working prototype
- Iterating without friction or fear of failure
- Following curiosity instead of debugging stress

You're not fighting the tools — you're *playing* with them.

🧘 How to Know You're in the Flow:

- You're writing **prompts**, not searching Stack Overflow.
- You're excited, not overwhelmed.
- You're thinking in **features**, not files.
- You lose track of time — in the best way possible.

⚡ Real-World Mini Projects Built in Flow

Let's look at what vibe coding can do when you let go of perfection and just *build*.

✦ 1. "Daily Vibes" Journal Web App

Prompt:

```
Create a simple journal app with a text area to enter
thoughts, a save button, and a list below showing all
past entries. Use localStorage. Keep the UI clean.
```

Within seconds, the AI returns:

- A working HTML/CSS/JS setup
- Connected storage
- Editable entries
- Responsive design

Total time to MVP: **20 minutes**
No frameworks. No fuss. Just flow.

🎧 2. AI-Powered Playlist Generator

Prompt:

```
Build a React app that asks for a user's mood and
returns a playlist of 10 songs from a mock API.
```

AI responds with:

- A functional UI
- A mocked data array
- Mood detection logic (bonus)
- Clean layout with TailwindCSS

Total time: **1 hour to full prototype**

Add ChatGPT API integration later? Easy. You're vibing.

✏️ 3. Bug Reporter Widget for a Website

Prompt:

```
Make a floating button on the bottom-right of a webpage
that opens a modal. Inside, there's a form for users to
describe bugs and submit them. Store in localStorage.
```

The AI delivers:

- A floating FAB-style button
- A modal overlay
- A form with validation
- JSON storage of reports

Instant feature. No library setup. Just the *vibe*.

⬣ Avoiding Analysis Paralysis & Overengineering

Vibe coding removes a ton of friction — but it also tempts you to do too much, too soon.

⃠ The Common Traps:

- Obsessing over frameworks ("Should I use React or Vue?")
- Getting stuck in prompt perfection ("What if this one isn't perfect?")
- Premature scaling ("Should I use microservices for this button?")

▪ How to Stay Flow-Focused:

- Start ugly. You can clean it later.
- Use mock data. Hook in APIs later.
- Focus on *function*, not structure.
- Treat AI like a sketchpad — it's okay to iterate.

Flow coding is about *moving*, not *perfecting*.

🎨 Coding as Creative Expression

Here's the beautiful part no one talks about enough:

> **Code is a canvas.**
> And with AI, more people can paint on it than ever before.

You don't need to memorize syntax to express your idea. You don't need to set up a whole project just to test something cool. You just need:

- A problem worth solving
- A clear idea
- A prompt

Then let your creativity take over.

You can code like an artist, sketching and refining.
You can build for fun again, not just functionality.

And that — more than any productivity hack — is the *real magic* of vibe coding.

⬛ Chapter Recap

- Flow state is where creativity and momentum merge
- Vibe coding puts you there faster — by skipping setup and focusing on intention
- Small projects, built fast, show how powerful the flow can be
- Avoid overengineering — ship first, scale later
- Let coding be your *creative outlet*, not just your job

🚀 Up Next: Chapter 7 — *Setting Up Your AI Stack*

Now that you're in the zone, let's get practical. Next, we'll walk through how to set up your dev environment with AI tools so you can stay in flow with minimal friction — no matter your experience level.

PART III: TOOLS, TRICKS, AND TEMPLATES

Chapter 7: Setting Up Your AI Stack

"Your tools shape your flow. Set them up right, and the vibe takes care of itself."

▉ Why Your Stack Matters

In vibe coding, your **setup is your studio**. Like a musician with the right instruments or a painter with the right brushes, the right dev environment helps you move faster, think clearer, and stay in flow.

This chapter will help you:

- Choose the right tools for your workflow
- Set them up to minimize friction
- Combine them in smart ways
- Automate repetitive stuff so you can focus on the creative work

Let's build your stack.

✖ Step 1: Choose Your Core Environment

Here's the big choice:

> **Do you want to code in a desktop IDE or in the browser?**

▉ Option A: Local IDEs (VS Code, Cursor)

◆ VS Code + GitHub Copilot

- 🗨 Great for: Traditional devs, full project control
- ✖ Add-ons: GitHub Copilot, Codeium, ChatGPT extension
- 💡 Tip: Use **code snippets + terminal** inside VS Code for full-stack builds

⚡ Cursor (AI-native editor)

- 🗨 Great for: Refactoring, debugging, inline prompting
- ✦ Features: In-editor AI chat, context awareness, edit with prompt
- 💡 Tip: Use Cursor's "Ask" feature to iterate on complex codebases

⊕ Option B: Browser-Based Setups

🗨 Replit Ghostwriter

- 🔥 Best for: Quick builds, beginners, live collaboration
- ✖ Tools: Browser-based IDE, terminal, AI assistant built-in
- 💡 Tip: Great for trying new ideas fast or sharing demos

💡 bolt.new & lovable.dev

- 🗨 Best for: Instant apps from prompts (with or without code)
- 💡 Tip: Use bolt for full-stack prototypes, lovable.dev for UI-first builds

🗨 Step 2: Use Multiple LLMs for Better Output

Every model has its strengths. Smart vibe coders **mix and match models** depending on the task.

Model	Best For
ChatGPT (OpenAI)	General reasoning, conversational coding
Claude (Anthropic)	Summarizing, long context, big-picture logic
Copilot (OpenAI)	Inline code, patterns, quick suggestions
Cody (Sourcegraph)	Navigating large codebases, smart search
Replit Ghostwriter	Simple syntax, great for beginners

■ Vibe Strategy: Model Swapping

- Plan with **ChatGPT**
- Build with **Copilot**
- Refactor with **Claude**
- Review with **Cody**

You're not locked in — you're orchestrating multiple voices.

🧩 Step 3: Must-Have Plugins & Extensions

🔧 VS Code Plugins:

- **GitHub Copilot** – Your inline AI partner
- **ChatGPT - CodeGPT** – Ask anything from inside VS Code
- **Codeium** – Free autocomplete AI

- **Better Comments** – Make your prompts + feedback clearer
- **REST Client** – Test APIs without leaving VS Code

⚡ Cursor Add-ons:

- Built-in Copilot
- One-click AI explanations and refactors

🛠 Replit Add-ons:

- Built-in version control
- Database integration
- Ghostwriter autocomplete

⬛ Step 4: Automate the Repetitive Stuff

✦ Suggested Automations:

What	Tool	How
Generate README	ChatGPT / Claude	Prompt: "Create a README for this project."
Auto-create tests	Copilot / GPT	Prompt: "Write Jest tests for this function."
Refactor entire files	Cursor / Claude	Use inline or copy-paste with "Refactor this for clarity."
Code search + summary	Cody	"Explain what this file does in plain English."

Use your AI like a *junior dev* who's always ready to help with the boring stuff.

🚀 Bonus: Add AI to Your CLI

If you're a terminal-first dev, try these:

- `aicommits` – Use AI to write commit messages from diffs
- `gptcli` – Ask GPT anything from your terminal
- `continue.dev` – Open-source VS Code extension for running local LLMs

These tools help bring AI power to where you already work — no context-switching required.

⬛ Sample AI Stack for a Vibe Coder

🎬 Local Dev (Full Stack)

- **Editor**: Cursor
- **AI Models**: ChatGPT + Claude + Copilot
- **Plugins**: REST Client, Prettier, GitLens
- **Workflow**: Prompt, build, refactor, document — all inline

🌐 Browser Dev (Fast Prototyping)

- **Platform**: Replit + Ghostwriter
- **Models**: Built-in + external ChatGPT tab
- **Workflow**: Sketch app ideas, code fast, share live links

🛠️ No-Code / Low-Code Dev

- **Platform**: lovable.dev

- **Workflow**: Drag UI, prompt AI for logic, deploy in minutes

■ Chapter Recap

- Choose your environment: local (VS Code/Cursor) or browser (Replit/bolt.new)
- Use multiple models for better outcomes — each has a vibe
- Install key extensions to streamline your flow
- Automate the boring stuff — let AI handle commits, docs, tests
- Treat your stack like a creative studio — dial in your tools to match your style

🚀 Up Next: Chapter 8 — *Code by Conversation: Use Cases in Action*

You've got the tools. Now it's time to **see what they can actually do**. In the next chapter, we'll walk through real coding scenarios — from building APIs to styling UIs — and show how AI steps in to speed things up, smooth things out, and help you ship more, faster.

Chapter 8: Code by Conversation — Use Cases in Action

"Your idea is the input. The code is the output. The conversation is the bridge."

⚔ Use Case 1: CRUD Apps and REST APIs

Let's start with the bread-and-butter of web dev: **CRUD apps** (Create, Read, Update, Delete).

With AI, you can go from zero to functional API in minutes.

✏ Example Prompt:

```
Create a REST API using Express.js that manages a list
of books. Each book should have an ID, title, author,
and published year. Use in-memory storage.
```

Result:

- Express server with GET, POST, PUT, DELETE routes
- Input validation
- JSON responses

- Starter data array

- "Add error handling for invalid IDs."
- "Make sure no book has a blank title."
- "Generate OpenAPI docs for this API."

The flow is iterative — and fun.
You're **building** by **describing**.

🟡 Use Case 2: Front-End Magic (React, Vue, Svelte)

Building front-ends with AI feels like giving your wireframes a voice.

Let's say you're working in **React**:

🎧 Prompt:

```
Build a React component for a user profile card that
displays a name, photo, and bio. Use TailwindCSS for
styling.
```

Output:

- A clean React component
- Properly structured props
- Tailwind layout

- Responsive design

Want to switch frameworks? Easy:

🌀 Prompt Remix:

```
Now rewrite this in Vue 3 using Composition API.
```

Or:

```
Convert this to a Svelte component with scoped styles.
```

Boom — cross-framework fluidity with just a sentence.

▌ Use Case 3: Mobile Apps (React Native, Flutter)

Yes, you can vibe code mobile apps too.

➔▌ Prompt:

```
Create a React Native app with a home screen showing a
welcome message and a button that navigates to a second
screen displaying a motivational quote.
```

AI gives you:

- Two screens
- Stack navigation setup
- Basic layout and styling

You can do the same in **Flutter**:

◎ **Prompt:**

```
Create a Flutter app with a bottom navigation bar and
two tabs: Home and Settings. Each tab should have its
own widget and icon.
```

AI provides:

- Full Dart code
- `BottomNavigationBar` with routes
- Stateful widgets
- Placeholder UIs ready for customization

You're building cross-platform apps like you're ordering lunch.

🌐 Use Case 4: Full-Stack Builds (bolt.new, lovable.dev)

For makers, founders, and solo hackers — AI-native platforms like **bolt.new** and **lovable.dev** can turn prompts into production-grade apps.

🚀 bolt.new Example:

Prompt:

```
Build a web app where users can submit anonymous
confessions. It should include a form, a list of past
entries, and an admin view to delete submissions. Use
PostgreSQL.
```

Result:

- Auth system
- DB schema
- Admin panel
- Working deployment URL

One prompt. Whole product.

💡 lovable.dev Example:

Prompt:

```
Create a landing page for a productivity tool with a
hero section, feature grid, pricing table, and
newsletter signup. Make it mobile-first and clean.
```

Result:

- Pixel-perfect UI
- Editable design
- Backend hookup with prompt guidance

- Instant shareable link

No code required — but code optional.

✏️ Use Case 5: Docs, Tests, and Data Mocks (Auto-Gen Everything)

Vibe coders don't write tests first — they **describe what should be tested**, and let AI generate it.

◼ Testing Prompt:

```
Write unit tests using Jest for this login function.
Include success and failure cases.
[Paste function]
```

AI delivers:

- Clear, readable test suite
- Proper use of describe and it blocks
- Edge case coverage

◼ Docs Prompt:

```
Write a README for this Node.js project that includes
setup instructions, API usage, and contribution
guidelines.
```

AI response:

- Markdown-formatted README
- Descriptions of endpoints
- Code examples and CLI usage

✏️ Mock Data Prompt:

```
Generate an array of 10 fake user objects with IDs,
names, emails, and profile images using JavaScript.
```

Instant result:

```
[
  {
    id: 1,
    name: "Jordan Steele",
    email: "jordan@example.com",
    avatar:
"https://randomuser.me/api/portraits/men/1.jpg"
  },
  ...
]
```

Perfect for:

- Prototypes
- UI design
- Local testing

🔥 Final Takeaway

Vibe coding isn't about skipping steps — it's about speeding up the ones that slow you down.
From building real apps to filling in all the details (tests, docs, mock data), you're now building **by conversation**, not configuration.

The result?
You can go from idea → demo → deploy in hours, not weeks.

⬛ Chapter Recap

- CRUD APIs and UI components are just a prompt away
- React, Vue, Svelte — AI can switch between frameworks easily
- Mobile dev is now conversational
- Tools like bolt.new and lovable.dev turn prompts into production
- Docs, tests, and mock data can all be generated automatically

🚀 Up Next: Chapter 9 — *Debugging with a Digital Sidekick*

Next, we're going to tackle bugs, errors, and spaghetti logic — and how your AI copilot can help untangle the mess, explain what's going wrong, and even write the fix for you.

Chapter 9: Debugging with a Digital Sidekick

"AI doesn't get frustrated. It just keeps trying. That's exactly what you want in a debugging partner."

Using AI to Find and Explain Bugs

Debugging has always been one of the most frustrating parts of programming. You hit a wall, stare at the error, and go into Stack Overflow survival mode.

But vibe coding gives you a new option:

You ask the AI what's wrong. And it tells you.

✏️ Example Prompt:

```
Here's a function that throws an error: "undefined is
not a function."
Can you help me debug it?
[Paste function code]
```

AI Response:

- Reads the code

- Pinpoints the problem (maybe you're calling `.map()` on a non-array)
- Explains *why* it fails
- Offers a corrected version

No guesswork. No ego. Just clear, fast feedback.

🧠 Why This Works:

- LLMs are great at **pattern recognition**
- They don't get tired or annoyed
- They explain in plain English — perfect for beginners or mid-level devs

🧠 Teaching the AI Your Code Context

Debugging is more than isolated lines — it's about **context**.

To get the best help from your AI sidekick, give it more to work with:

◼ Prompt:

```
You're helping me debug a React app.
Here's my state management setup:
[Paste Redux slice or context code]
And here's the component that's breaking:
[Paste component code]
The error says: "Cannot read properties of undefined
(reading 'length')"
```

Now the AI has:

- The logic
- The error
- The component flow

And it can offer a much **deeper analysis**, like:

- "Looks like you're calling `.length` on `props.items`, but `items` is never passed down."
- "You could add a default prop or conditional check."

🔋 Code Smells, Refactors, and Performance Tuning

Your AI assistant can also act like a **code reviewer**, spotting things you might miss.

💡 Prompt:

```
Can you review this function for readability and
performance?
What could be improved?
[Paste code]
```

The AI might flag:

- Deeply nested logic

- Duplicate code
- Unused variables
- Inefficient loops
- API calls inside render functions (oops)

🗨 Prompt for Refactoring:

```
Refactor this code to be more modular and readable.
```

Or:

```
Rewrite this function using ES6 syntax and cleaner
structure.
```

It's like pair programming, but the pair is a nonjudgmental robot who just wants you to write cleaner code.

🪄 Staying in Control — When AI Goes Rogue

Okay — now the real talk.

AI isn't perfect. It can:

- Suggest solutions that don't compile
- "Hallucinate" functions that don't exist
- Miss subtle logic errors
- Overcomplicate a simple fix

That's why **you're still the conductor.**
Use AI to **explore, clarify,** and **inspire** — not as the final judge.

🔴 Red Flags to Watch For:

Symptom	What It Might Mean
Code compiles but breaks behavior	Logic drift or misunderstood context
AI adds code that doesn't exist	Hallucination (fake methods or APIs)
Response is too confident, but wrong	Always test before trusting
Repeats boilerplate unnecessarily	Needs tighter, more scoped prompts

🧘 What To Do:

- Ask it to explain its changes
- Rerun the same prompt with tighter scope
- Try a second LLM (Claude or ChatGPT with different tone)
- Break large problems into smaller pieces

AI works best when you **collaborate,** not delegate.

⚙️ Debugging Prompt Toolkit

Goal	Example Prompt
Find a bug	"This throws a TypeError. Can you help me fix it?"
Explain an error message	"Explain this error like I'm new: 'Cannot read properties of undefined.'"
Refactor messy logic	"Make this cleaner and easier to read."
Improve performance	"Can you optimize this loop?"
Validate AI's fix	"Are you sure this won't break anything?"

◼ Chapter Recap

- AI can help identify and explain bugs quickly
- Give your assistant context for better results
- Use it to refactor, optimize, and clean up code
- But don't outsource all the trust — **test everything**
- Stay in the loop — you're still the architect of the system

🚀 Up Next: Chapter 10 — *Start with Just an Idea*

In the next chapter, we'll show how you can go from a pure idea — scribbled on a napkin or described in a single sentence — to a full working project using AI tools. It's where your creative side meets real results.

PART IV: BUILDING AND SHIPPING IN THE AI ERA

Chapter 10: Start with Just an Idea

"The barrier to entry is no longer code — it's clarity."

💡 Building Apps from Pure Language

You no longer need a CS degree, a stack of textbooks, or a week-long sprint to build software.

All you need is an idea and the ability to express it clearly.

With tools like **ChatGPT**, **bolt.new**, **Cursor**, and **lovable.dev**, you can start with a sentence and end with a working app — sometimes in under an hour.

This flips the entire development model:

- From **code-first** → to **vision-first**
- From "How do I build this?" → to "What am I trying to create?"

Vibe coding is about sketching your software in words — then refining it, piece by piece.

🧠 From Whiteboard to Working Prototype

Let's walk through the new workflow:

Step 1: The Spark

Write out what you want to build — like you're telling a friend over coffee.

> "I want to build an app where people can anonymously confess stuff. No accounts, just a form and a feed of entries."

Step 2: The Prompt

Feed that into an AI tool (ChatGPT, bolt.new, or Cursor):

```
Create a simple full-stack web app where users can
submit anonymous confessions.
It should include a text input form, a submit button,
and a feed that displays recent confessions.
Use in-memory storage for now, no login required. Make
it mobile-friendly.
```

Step 3: AI Generates Your MVP

- Frontend form and feed
- Backend endpoints (POST + GET)
- Styling with Tailwind or plain CSS
- Deployable in-browser (Replit) or locally with Node

You just built an app — in a few prompts.

🖌 Project Walkthrough: A To-Do App (With a Twist)

Let's show this in real time with a familiar example — but with a little creativity.

🔴 Goal:

A to-do app with:

- Tasks
- Due dates
- A motivational quote every time you check something off

Step 1: Prompt the Base App

```
Create a to-do list web app using HTML, CSS, and
JavaScript.
Users should be able to add tasks, mark them complete,
and remove them.
Store tasks in localStorage.
```

AI Returns:

- Task form
- List rendering
- Completion logic
- Persistent localStorage

Step 2: Add the Twist

> Every time a user checks off a task, display a random
> motivational quote below the list.
> Use a built-in array of 10 quotes.

AI Adds:

- `quotes[]` array
- Event listener on checkboxes
- Display area for the quote

Step 3: Polish the UI

> Make the app mobile-friendly with responsive styling.
> Use a soft color palette and rounded elements for a
> calm, motivating vibe.

Boom — you now have a full-featured, creative app.

Want to deploy it?

> Add instructions on how to deploy this app to GitHub
> Pages.

AI gives you the steps.

 Teaching Non-Devs to Launch with AI

This is the real revolution.

People who:

- Thought they couldn't code
- Never touched an IDE
- Have killer ideas but no dev budget

Can now:

- Describe their vision
- Get working code
- Launch prototypes in a day

💬 Example:

Your cousin wants a site for their food truck. They describe what they want over text.

You feed that into ChatGPT:

```
Create a one-page responsive website for a taco truck
called "Spicy Bites."
Include sections for menu, location, hours, and a photo
gallery. Use bright colors and playful fonts.
```

In a minute, you've got the code.
They have a website.
They're in business.

▮ Platforms Perfect for Non-Devs

Tool	Why It Works
bolt.new	Turns plain language into full-stack apps

lovable.dev	Visual builder with AI backend wiring
Replit + Ghostwriter	Low-friction browser IDE, perfect for experimentation
ChatGPT	Explains every step, offers edits, and holds your hand through setup

---

■ Chapter Recap

- You can build real apps starting with **just an idea**
- Prompts = the new wireframes
- AI can help scaffold, style, and deploy
- Non-coders can launch products, sites, and tools
- Vibe coding democratizes development — clarity of vision is now the superpower

🚀 Up Next: Chapter 11 — *Scaling the Vibe: Big Projects, Small Teams*

Next, we're going beyond MVPs. You'll learn how vibe coding works at scale — with bigger apps, more files, more logic — and how AI helps small teams do the work of many without sacrificing clarity or quality.

Chapter 11: Scaling the Vibe — Big Projects, Small Teams

"When AI handles the grunt work, your small team can move like a startup and think like a studio."

🤖 AI as a Junior Dev, Mentor, and PM

Once your project grows beyond a single feature or prototype, it's easy to get overwhelmed by:

- Code organization
- Technical debt
- Versioning
- Collaboration

Here's where AI steps up — wearing **multiple hats** depending on how you prompt it.

⬤ AI as a Junior Developer

- 🛠 Writes boilerplate, hooks, utilities
- ✏️ Generates tests, config files, build scripts
- ⬛ Follows your lead, fast and reliably

  Prompt:
   "Create a reusable function that formats a date into 'Month Day, Year'. Add unit tests."

🗣 AI as a Mentor

- 💬 Explains unfamiliar code
- 💬 Suggests better patterns
- ■ Offers feedback on architecture

Prompt:
"Can you explain this React context setup to me? I want to understand how state flows."

📋 AI as a Project Manager

- 📌 Breaks tasks into chunks
- ■ Suggests a roadmap
- ■ Helps manage scope creep

Prompt:
"I'm building a multi-user recipe app. What features should I include in v1? Can you organize them by priority?"

AI isn't just a coding assistant — it's an **alignment tool**.

🔍 Managing Scope and Versioning with AI

Scope creep is a vibe killer — but AI can help you **keep projects lean and maintainable**.

📁 Prompt Example:

```
Help me break this app idea into v1, v2, and future
features.
Make sure v1 stays minimal and functional.
```

You get:

- A prioritized feature list
- A clear MVP scope
- A sanity check for overengineering

Now for versioning:

Prompt:
"Write a changelog entry for the latest feature: added user
authentication with JWT."

Bonus: Ask AI to **generate migration scripts**, rollback steps, or test
coverage checks.

🏗 Scaffolding, Component Generation, and Modular Design

Big projects need structure. Luckily, AI's great at scaffolding — and it
never forgets to close a div.

◼ Prompt: Scaffolding a Project

```
Scaffold a full-stack blog platform with:
- A React frontend
- Node/Express backend
```

```
- MongoDB database
- Auth routes and protected pages
```

You'll get:

- File structure
- API route templates
- Frontend page stubs
- Auth middleware

You're not starting from scratch — you're starting **halfway in**.

🎨 Prompt: Component Generation

```
Generate a reusable modal component in React that
accepts a title, body, and confirm/cancel callbacks.
Style it with Tailwind.
```

Boom — reusable, clean, and fast.

Want modularity?

> **Prompt:**
> "Split this 400-line component into smaller child
> components and move them into a components/
> directory."

The AI keeps you organized — and saves your future self from pain.

🪱 Team Workflows When Everyone's Vibing

Vibe coding isn't just a solo thing. Teams can benefit massively — if you set up **clear AI workflows**.

🟥 Team Flow Blueprint:

Role	AI Use
Designer	Prompts UI components into React/Vue/Svelte
Frontend Dev	Prompts layout logic, form handling, validation
Backend Dev	Prompts API routes, data models, tests
PM/Product	Prompts docs, changelogs, roadmap drafts
QA	Prompts test suites and mocks for various states

Each team member becomes a **vibe conductor** in their own lane — but they're all working from the same AI-powered orchestra.

✨ Pro Tip: Shared Prompt Docs

Keep a `prompt-recipes.md` file in your repo:

- "Generate tests for X"
- "Explain logic in Y"
- "Create docs for Z"

This keeps your **AI workflows repeatable and scalable** across teammates.

🛶 **Collaboration Stack:**

Tool	Role in Team Workflow
Cursor	AI code editing across the whole repo
ChatGPT (team access)	Ideation, planning, debugging
bolt.new	MVP staging and experimentation
Replit	Easy demos, shared live coding
GitHub Copilot	Inline acceleration for all devs
Claude or Cody	Summarizing, documenting, reviewing codebase logic

⬛ Chapter Recap

- AI can wear many hats: dev, mentor, PM
- It helps break down features and scope like a pro
- Scaffolding and modular prompts speed up project structure
- Teams that share AI workflows stay aligned and move faster
- The more intentional your prompts, the more scalable your flow

🚀 Up Next: Chapter 12 — *Deploy, Launch, Repeat*

Shipping used to be the scariest part. Now it's just another conversation. In the next chapter, we'll talk about launching your AI-assisted builds, automating deployments, writing changelogs, and releasing updates — all without leaving the vibe.

Chapter 12: Deploy, Launch, Repeat

"If you can ship it, you can shape it. And now you can ship faster than ever."

AI-Assisted Deployment and CI/CD

Traditionally, deployment was the part of the project where things fell apart:

- Environment configs
- Build scripts
- CI pipelines
- Weird production bugs

But with AI? It's like having a DevOps engineer who *never gets annoyed*.

🔧 Prompt: Basic Deploy Workflow

```
Give me step-by-step instructions to deploy a Node.js +
React app to Vercel.
```

You get:

- Instructions for both frontend and backend

- `vercel.json` config files
- Environment variable setup
- Git-based deploy steps

Want Docker?

```
Generate a Dockerfile for this app and a
docker-compose.yml to run it with MongoDB.
```

You now have full containerized deployment — no trial-and-error needed.

🔧 Popular Platforms That Play Well with AI:

Platform	Use
Vercel	Frontend & full-stack deployment
Netlify	JAMstack, static sites, serverless functions
Render	Backend hosting with databases
Fly.io	Fast, globally distributed apps
Replit	One-click live apps, great for prototypes
Glitch	Collaborative real-time app building

⬢ Packaging, Shipping, and Marketing with AI

Launch isn't just tech. You also need:

- A landing page
- A product description
- A changelog
- Maybe even a tweet

🤖 Prompt: Product Copy

```
Write a fun, conversational product description for an
app that helps freelancers track time, with built-in
Pomodoro timers.
```

🤖 Prompt: Social Launch

```
Create a Twitter thread to announce my new AI-powered
journaling app. Keep it chill but informative.
```

The AI can write:

- Tweets
- Headlines
- CTAs
- FAQs

It's not just your dev partner — it's your **launch team**.

⬛ Maintaining and Evolving Your Product

Shipping isn't the end — it's the beginning.

Your users will give feedback. Features will evolve. Bugs will sneak in. Luckily, you now have an AI that helps you iterate at speed.

🧩 Feature Iteration Prompt

```
Users are asking for a dark mode. Help me add theme
switching to this React app with TailwindCSS.
```

🧪 Maintenance Prompt

```
Audit this codebase for deprecated packages and
outdated dependencies.
```

AI helps:

- Plan updates
- Fix regressions
- Write upgrade guides

You stay focused on vision — AI keeps the system running smooth.

● Building in Public — With Your AI Copilot

Vibe coding isn't just efficient — it's also a perfect match for **building in public**.

Why?

- You can move fast and show progress
- You can document your build process *as* you go (with AI help)
- You can engage your audience in real time

💬 Use AI to Help You:

Task	Prompt
📣 Weekly update post	"Write a LinkedIn post summarizing this week's progress on my open-source finance tracker."
🎞 Visual teaser	"Suggest a layout for a teaser screenshot for this journaling app."
🛠 Devlog	"Generate a devlog entry for the new feature: multi-language support for onboarding."

When you share your journey, the AI helps you tell the story.

📣 Tools for Building in Public:

- **X (Twitter)**: Threads, product updates, launch hype
- **LinkedIn**: Devlogs and longer progress updates
- **Substack or Medium**: Build story and project philosophy
- **Product Hunt**: AI can help you prepare your launch copy and assets

■ Chapter Recap

- You can deploy fast with AI guiding config, hosting, and pipelines
- AI helps you write everything you need for launch — not just code
- Maintenance becomes less painful — AI handles the low-level grunt work
- Building in public? AI can write the posts, polish the pitch, and amplify your story

🚀 Up Next: Chapter 13 — *Will Everyone Be a Developer?*

In the next chapter, we zoom way out. If anyone can build with language… what does that mean for the future of dev work, tech careers, and how we define what it means to be "a developer"?

We're not done. The ripple effects of vibe coding are just beginning.

PART V: WHERE WE'RE HEADED

Chapter 13: Will Everyone Be a Developer?

"When everyone can build with words, the definition of a 'developer' changes forever."

● The Democratization of Coding

We're living through a seismic shift.

Coding — once a specialized skill reserved for people with years of training — is becoming **a creative medium** accessible to anyone who can think clearly and write with intent.

- You don't need to memorize syntax
- You don't need to choose between 50 frameworks
- You don't even need to install anything

You just need to **describe** what you want.

Code is no longer the entry point — **language is.**

That means:

- Artists can build apps
- Writers can build tools
- Teachers can build platforms
- Entrepreneurs can launch products — solo

This isn't just a tech transformation. It's a cultural one.

● Devs as Product Designers, Strategists, and Artists

So where does this leave *developers* — the people who've been in the trenches for years?

It levels them *up*.

Vibe coders aren't losing control — they're gaining creative range.

You go from:

- Writing glue code → to designing the **experience**
- Solving syntax errors → to solving **real problems**
- Chasing the "right" abstraction → to shaping **clearer outcomes**

The New Developer Roles:

Old Role	New Vibe
Code typist	Product thinker
Framework ninja	System architect
Bug fixer	Creative guide
Tech translator	Language shaper
Siloed engineer	Multidisciplinary builder

AI doesn't replace developers — it **amplifies** the ones who know how to think clearly, test ideas fast, and zoom out to the big picture.

⊚ When the Line Between Code and Idea Disappears

This is the wild part.

We're entering a future where **you describe what you want**, and it becomes real:

- "Build me a multiplayer word game."
- "Spin up a dashboard that tracks my crypto portfolio."
- "Make a budgeting app that texts me when I overspend."

No dev handoff. No design mockups. No requirements doc.
Just a **conversation** between your brain and the machine.

That Changes Everything:

- MVPs don't take months — they take **minutes**
- People who never touched code can solve **problems on their own**
- Developers stop doing **manual labor**, and start doing **intent architecture**

💬 So... Will Everyone Be a Developer?

Yes — but not in the way you think.

The word *developer* used to mean:

"Someone who writes code."

Now it means:

"Someone who builds digital things."

In that sense?
Yes. Everyone will become a kind of developer.

- Kids building games with prompts
- Creators scripting interactivity into their portfolios
- Small business owners automating their workflows
- Coaches designing their own mobile apps

If you have an idea — and a few good prompts — **you can build**.

That's the new default.

🗣 What's Next for Devs?

Some people fear AI will make developers irrelevant. But the truth?

Devs who vibe with AI will become the most powerful builders in history.

They'll:

- Launch more
- Iterate faster
- Invent new genres of software
- Collaborate across design, marketing, and business
- Teach others how to think like builders — not just coders

The future is wide open. And you're already ahead of it.

■ Chapter Recap

- Coding is no longer gatekept — it's being democratized by AI
- Developers are evolving into **creative, strategic technologists**
- Code and intent are merging into one creative flow
- "Developer" is becoming a **mindset**, not a job title
- Anyone with ideas can now be a builder — that's the new reality

🚀 Up Next: Chapter 14 — *Staying Human in an AI World*

Before we wrap, let's talk about the ethics, limits, and human intuition that still matter deeply in this new era. AI is powerful — but it's not perfect. The human touch? Still irreplaceable.

Chapter 14: Staying Human in an AI World

"AI can write code, but it can't feel the problem you're solving. That's still your superpower."

🛑 Guardrails, Ethics, and Hallucinations

AI tools are incredibly helpful — but they're not perfect. And when you're shipping software with them, you have to **know the risks**.

✦ Hallucinations

LLMs sometimes:

- Invent functions or APIs that don't exist
- Generate code that looks correct but doesn't run
- Fabricate fake package names, imports, or references

They're not trying to trick you — they're **guessing based on patterns**.

Prompt:

```
Write a secure user login flow in Node.js.
```

AI might return:

- A solid structure
- Or an insecure one (e.g. storing passwords in plain text)

That's why **testing, validation, and basic security awareness** still matter.

⬤ Ethics & Guardrails

As AI gets more powerful, so do the questions:

- Who owns the code it generates?
- What happens if it recreates someone else's work?
- Can you trust its recommendations when they impact real people?

You're not just coding. You're shaping **experiences** and, in some cases, **livelihoods**.

> Use AI, but don't surrender your judgment.

🔐 Open Source, IP, and Trust

The legal landscape around AI-generated code is still developing.

Some questions to consider:

- If Copilot suggests a GPL-licensed function, do you have to comply with GPL?
- If your app uses AI-generated logic, who owns the IP?
- Can you trust what it pulls in from training data?

The truth is: **we don't fully know yet**. But here's what you *can* do right now:

■ **Smart Practices:**

Action	Why It Helps
Run license checks	Avoid accidental copyright issues
Credit your sources	Keep your work transparent
Use AI to explain code	Understand what you're shipping
Double-check "magic" solutions	Verify that shortcuts are safe

The tools are fast — but **you're still the gatekeeper.**

● Why Your Taste, Intuition, and Imagination Still Matter

Here's the thing AI can't do:

- It doesn't **feel** the user's pain point
- It doesn't know when the UX is awkward
- It doesn't sense when something feels off, bloated, or just plain boring

That's you. Your **human intuition.**

You still need to:

- Choose what to build
- Decide when it's "good enough"
- Know what your users need (sometimes before they do)
- Refine for elegance, clarity, or joy

AI is the engine. **You're the designer of the ride.**

🐸 Taste Still Wins

Plenty of people can build websites with AI.
But a few will build *delightful* ones.

Taste is knowing when to stop.
Imagination is knowing what doesn't exist yet.

That's not in the model. That's in *you*.

💜 Staying Human = Staying Curious

Being human in an AI world doesn't mean rejecting the tools.

It means:

- Asking better questions
- Thinking deeply about your choices
- Infusing your work with story, meaning, and craft
- Knowing when to trust your gut — even if the AI disagrees

AI can co-create. But **you set the tone**.

⬛ Chapter Recap

- AI isn't perfect — hallucinations, ethics, and security still matter
- Legal and IP issues around AI code are evolving — be aware and careful
- Your taste, vision, and emotional intelligence are still irreplaceable

- Being human means guiding the tech — not being guided by it
- Curiosity, empathy, and imagination are your edge

🚀 Up Next: Chapter 15 — *Your Vibe Coding Journey*

We're nearly there. In the final chapter, we'll look at how to keep learning, stay in flow, and evolve your skills in this fast-moving space — plus how to help others start their own journey into vibe coding.

Chapter 15: Your Vibe Coding Journey

"The tools will keep changing. Your mindset is what carries you forward."

✦ How to Stay Sharp, Inspired, and Evolving

Vibe coding isn't a one-time skill you "finish." It's a way of approaching creativity with code — and it evolves as you do.

The AI tools you use today will be different a year from now. But if you stay curious, adaptable, and experimental, you'll always be ahead of the curve.

Here's how to keep your edge:

🧠 Stay Sharp:

- **Keep prompting** — treat it like a muscle
- Try new tools and LLMs regularly
- Revisit old code and refactor with fresh eyes
- Ask *why* a suggestion works, not just *how*

🧠 Stay Inspired:

- Build weird stuff just for fun
- Remix prompts from other creators
- Follow devs who are vibing in public

- Share your builds — even when they're rough

The more you build, the more you learn.
The more you share, the more others grow.

🌐 Communities, Forums, and Resources

Vibe coding thrives in community. If you want to stay in the loop (and keep your flow going), plug into spaces where builders are constantly experimenting.

Here are a few to keep in your rotation:

📓 Where to Hang Out:

- **Twitter/X** → For dev threads, AI tool drops, and vibey launch energy
- **Reddit** → r/ChatGPT, r/ProgrammerHumor, r/webdev for inspo and hacks
- **Discord servers** → Many AI tools have thriving communities with live support and workflow ideas
- **YouTube & Twitch** → Live coding sessions and walkthroughs of vibe-built projects
- **Dev.to & Hashnode** → Long-form writeups, tutorials, and AI-driven dev logs

🍫 Keep Learning:

- OpenAI Cookbook
- Anthropic's Claude docs
- GitHub Copilot resources
- Prompt engineering guides (e.g., awesome-chatgpt-prompts repo)

💼 Building Your Own Workflows, Toolchains, and Habits

Now that you've got the fundamentals, your next move is to build a vibe coding workflow that's *yours*.

Start simple:

🛠 Example Personal Stack:

- **Editor**: Cursor (for prompt-driven code edits)
- **Copilot**: Inline dev flow
- **ChatGPT**: Brainstorming, planning, and problem solving
- **Claude**: Summarizing big code files
- **GitHub + Vercel**: Code + deploy

Then layer in **routines**:

Habit	Why it Helps
Prompt daily	Builds fluency in natural language coding
Ship weekly	Keeps your flow active and builds confidence
Share openly	Attracts feedback, opportunities, and collaborators
Save good prompts	Create your own "vibe recipe book" over time

Make your AI tools your creative team. Build rituals around your sessions. Stay curious. Stay fluid.

🌱 Keep Vibing — and Help Others Start, Too

You've made it through the journey. You've learned:

- How to prompt with clarity
- How to collaborate with AI tools
- How to ship apps from pure ideas
- How to work solo or with a small team
- How to keep your creative spark lit

Now it's your turn to help others step into the wave.

Share your workflows.
Teach your friends.
Post your prompts.
Build in public.
Answer questions.
Launch weird projects.
Let people see you in flow.

The future of software isn't gated behind complexity anymore. It's open. It's expressive. And it's human.

Vibe coding is **not just about faster code** — it's about more people having the power to build.

And the more people we bring into this mindset, the more we all win.

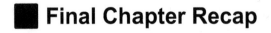 Final Chapter Recap

- Keep learning by building, prompting, and remixing
- Join communities to stay current and connected
- Build your own stack + habits to stay in flow
- Share your journey and help others start theirs
- The vibe isn't just a toolset — it's a movement

💬 One Last Prompt for You:

"What do you want to build next?"

Ask your tools. Ask your creativity. Ask your community.
Then go build it — and keep the vibe alive.

Appendices

A. Prompt Templates — Ready-to-Use Structures for Common Dev Tasks

These are plug-and-play templates you can use with ChatGPT, Claude, Cursor, or any other code-generating AI.

■ Scaffolding a Project

```
Scaffold a [frontend/backend/full-stack] app using
[React, Node, Svelte, etc.].
Include [authentication, CRUD endpoints, basic routing,
etc.].
Use [database or localStorage]. Keep the code
organized.
```

■ Writing Features

```
Build a feature in [framework/language] that lets users
[do X].
Include basic validation and a clean UI.
```

✎ Writing Tests

```
Write unit tests for this [function/component] using
[Jest/Vitest].
Cover both success and failure cases.
[Paste code here]
```

🖤 Refactoring

```
Refactor this code to improve readability, reduce
duplication, and use modern syntax.
Split it into smaller functions if needed.
```

🔧 Debugging

```
I'm getting this error: "[error message]."
Here's the code that's breaking.
Can you explain the issue and suggest a fix?
[Paste code]
```

◾ Writing Docs

```
Generate a README for this app.
It should include setup instructions, usage examples,
and API routes.
[Optional: Paste code or app description]
```

🖊 Creating Mock Data

```
Generate an array of 10 fake [users/products/tasks]
with fields: [name, email, etc.].
Use realistic but fake data.
```

B. Glossary of Terms

A quick-reference for the most common terms in vibe coding and AI development.

Term	Definition
LLM	Large Language Model — the AI models that generate code from natural language
Prompt	A request or instruction given to an AI
Prompt Engineering	Crafting prompts that result in better, more accurate AI responses
Prompt Chaining	Using a sequence of related prompts to refine or build upon AI outputs
Hallucination	When an AI makes something up (e.g. a fake function, incorrect answer)
Vibe Coding	A style of development where you build apps using plain language prompts
Refactor	Rewriting code to improve clarity or structure without changing its behavior
MVP	Minimum Viable Product — the simplest version of an app that delivers value

Scaffolding	Generating a project structure, file layout, or starter code
Flow State	A mental state of deep focus and momentum while creating or coding
Zero-to-App	The process of going from pure idea to deployed product using AI tools

C. 10 Projects to Try Right Now — Buildable in a Weekend with AI

1. **Confession Board**
   An anonymous message wall using localStorage and a simple Express backend.
2. **Motivational To-Do App**
   A task manager that shows a random quote every time you check something off.
3. **Weather Mood Tracker**
   An app that logs your mood along with the current weather — built with a weather API.
4. **AI Writing Assistant**
   A web-based tool that helps users brainstorm and generate content using the ChatGPT API.
5. **Habit Tracker**
   Track habits, visualize streaks, and store data in localStorage or Supabase.
6. **Personal Portfolio Generator**
   Use AI to build a dynamic, stylish portfolio from a text bio and resume.
7. **Simple Budget App**
   Add expenses and incomes, calculate totals, and display charts with Chart.js.

8. **Flashcard Quizzer**
   Create custom decks and test yourself using localStorage or a simple backend.
9. **Real-Time Polling App**
   Users create polls, vote live, and see instant results. (Try Socket.io + AI.)
10. **Voice Note Journal**
    Record short voice memos, transcribe them using AI, and store them for later review.

D. Resources & Communities — Where to Keep Learning and Connecting

🔲 Communities:

- r/ChatGPT – Prompt sharing, updates, and use cases
- Buildspace – Creator-focused learning with community
- Replit Discord – Live chat and collabs
- AI Engineer Weekly – Newsletter focused on AI toolchains and devs
- Dev.to – Great for reading, writing, and sharing technical blog posts

🔳 Learning Resources:

- OpenAI Cookbook
- Anthropic's Claude Docs
- Prompt Engineering Guide
- Awesome ChatGPT Prompts
- Cursor.dev Docs
- GitHub Copilot

💼 Tools Worth Bookmarking:

Tool	Link
ChatGPT	chat.openai.com
Claude	claude.ai
bolt.new	bolt.new
lovable.dev	lovable.dev
Cursor	cursor.so
Replit	replit.com
Codeium	codeium.com

Disclaimer:

This book was written with the assistance of AI tools, including AI-powered code generators, writing assistants, and research companions. While every effort has been made to ensure clarity, accuracy, and usefulness, readers should be aware that AI technologies evolve rapidly. As a result, some tools, workflows, or examples described in this book may become outdated or behave differently by the time of publication.

The content presented reflects the state of AI development at the time of writing. Readers are encouraged to explore the latest updates, documentation, and community discussions to stay current. Use this book as a starting point for your own experimentation—and remember, the best way to stay in the flow is to keep vibing and adapting.